This book belongs to:

_____

_____

_____

Many years ago, David was a young boy who loved watching television programmes, films and plays. David would put up his hand enthusiastically to take part in school productions and his parents came to see him perform in many shows. He would sometimes be the narrator of the story, or play a leading role on stage!

His Mummy, Daddy and siblings enjoyed seeing him perform.

He was not always the best dancer in his school productions, but he would practice the movements over and over again until he could perform his routines without making any mistakes.

David enjoyed watching his favourite films starring famous actors like, Whoopi Goldberg, Oprah Winfrey and Denzel Washington on television. He knew that when he grew up he wanted to be an actor just like them!

When David became a teenager, he began acting lessons at a local drama school, but his parents were unsure how many classes they could afford. They warned him that they could only pay for twenty lessons altogether.
This made David very worried.

He did some research and found he was able to earn a scholarship for young people who wanted to become actors. David completed an application for the scholarship and was successful because of glowing recommendations from his school and drama teachers.

He could go to drama lessons three times per week and this made him very happy!

David also enjoyed sports. He would play football with his two younger brothers and school friends, making sure that everyone was included. He knew that being active would keep him healthy and was a fun way to spend time with his friends.

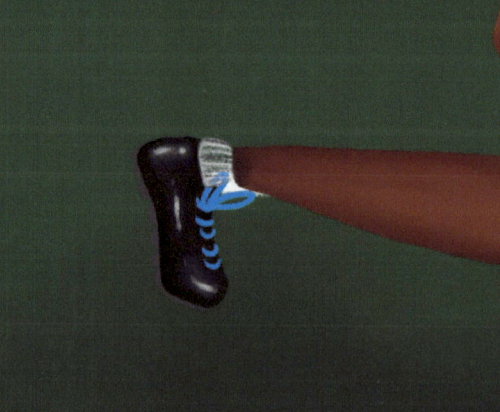

The college he went to did not have a drama course, but David had accomplished good grades in English, Maths and Geography. David began working in an office job, but he soon realised he wasn't feeling very fulfilled.

Each day seemed to be the same as the one before.

During office hours when he was on his break-times, David had a talent for speaking and would grab his colleagues' attention with accounts of the activities he had fulfilled with his family over the weekend.

In the evenings, David continued his drama classes. He often arrived at the theatre, before the caretaker Albert appeared. His bunch of keys jangled as he climbed the steps walked to open the doors.

15

Once inside, David would perform his physical warm-ups and practice his vocal exercises; his voice was clear, consistent in tone and projected across the theatre with its wooden floors and high ceilings.

David's drama teachers felt that he was very good at showing the emotions of sadness, happiness, enthusiasm and shock. David was good at making facial expressions and was able to convince the audience that his story was true to life.

David read many books and would bring endless stories to life in his mind. It helped him expand his vocabulary and use his imagination.

When he was given scripts for plays at drama school he was able to follow them and learn his lines quickly.

When David stood up to practise a scene in rehearsals, he was always the one who knew his lines best.

The teachers and fellow students always clapped and shouted enthusiastically when David performed a scene.

CLAP!
CLAP!
CLAP!

AMAZING!

WHOO!

WHOO!

David won awards for being the 'Best in Class' on many occasions. He hung the certificates on his bedroom wall and looked at them when he woke up in the mornings; he felt proud of his achievements!

David showed promise as an actor, he was from a small city in England with only two theatres in the town center.

He knew that if he wanted to embark on a professional career in acting he would have to go to the capital city of England, London...

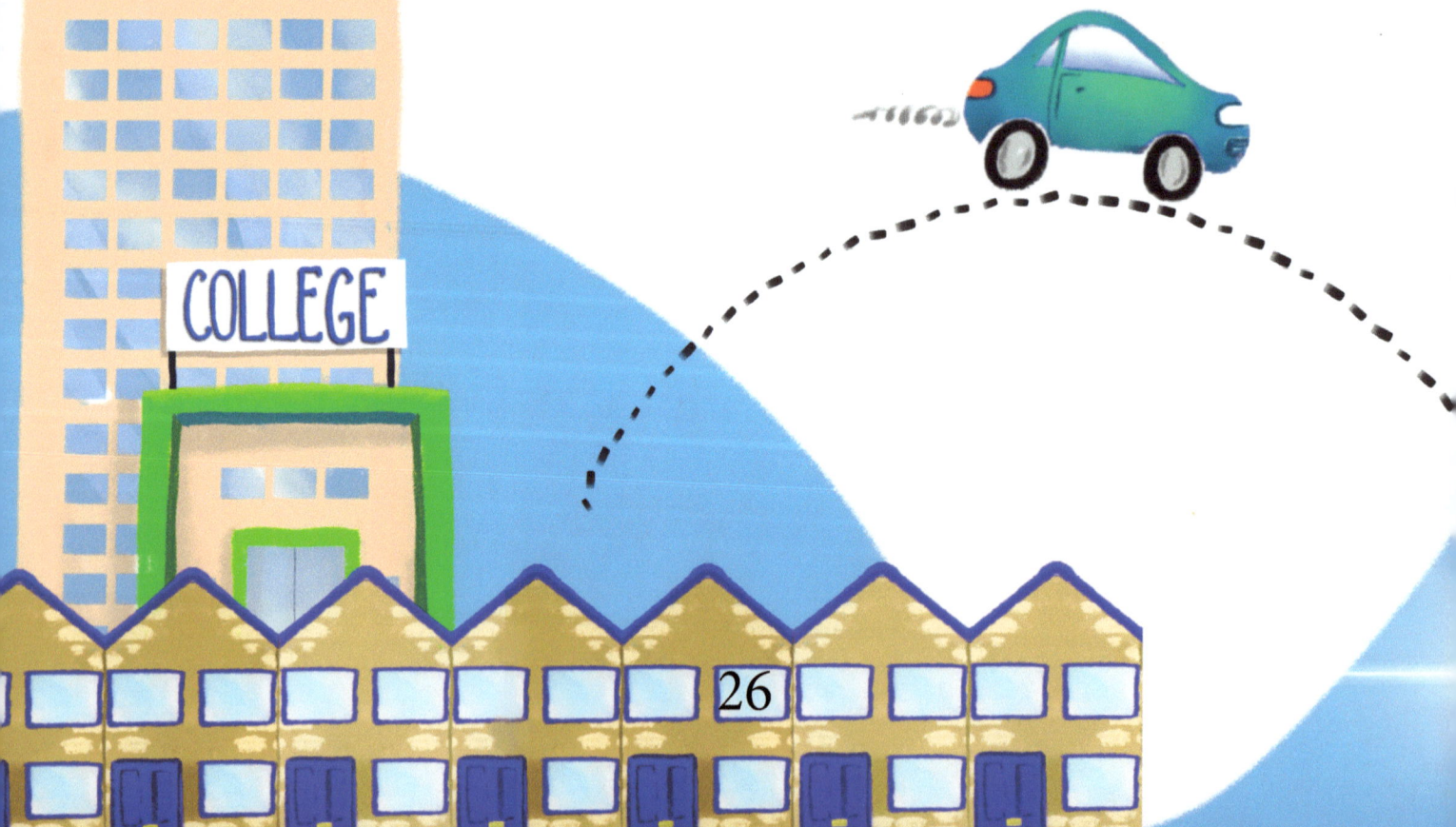

In London there were several well-known acting schools. Many world famous actors had trained in these institutions and travelled the globe to work in theatres and on film sets. They used their skills to bring to life stories and information - from historical dramas and science fiction to wildlife and political documentaries. David wanted to follow in the footsteps of those actors!

David enrolled at a large drama school and studied there for three years in his early twenties.

David took part in many amateur plays whilst completing his higher-level drama studies. Soon, he applied for his Equity Card which allowed him to be paid for his work.

He began auditioning professionally and earned small parts in a number of television series. This meant that he would appear on the small screen in people's homes week after week.

He also performed in plays on stage including the very famous Royal Shakespeare Company stage in Stratford-upon-Avon.

Eventually David travelled to America to play a main role in a famous television series which won international awards. He enjoyed sitting with famous celebrities and sometimes being nominated for awards.

David won so many awards for his performances!

35

David frequently came back from America to be with his family in England.

While in England he started creating documentaries to educate the public about difficulties some people face.

This helped improve the lives of those who were struggling with different issues. His research and sharing of information made things much better for them.

David's services to drama meant he was appointed a Member of the Order of the British Empire (MBE). Twelve years later, he was appointed as an Officer of the Order of the British Empire (OBE) as he has given services to drama and charity.

David has always been a very kind and generous person. When he became successful, he bought a new house for his family and helped his siblings enjoy amazing holidays.

David is now famous around the world.
He still encourages young people who enjoy acting to build their skills and confidence by taking drama lessons.

This means they can take part in school plays and audition for shows such as Annie, Matilda or The Lion King. Some children gain roles on TV in dramas and children's shows.

Acting gives them an opportunity to become familiar with the life of the theatre and the art of performance.

They too can become professional actors!

41

Maybe you would enjoy the opportunity and become as famous as Josette Simon, Idris Elba, Daniel Kaluuya, Chiwetel Ejiofor, Whoopi Goldberg and the long list of many other famous actors both in the UK, America and around the world.

43

Maybe you would enjoy the opportunity and become as famous as Josette Simon, Idris Elba, Daniel Kaluuya, Chiwetel Ejiofor, Whoopi Goldberg and the long list of many other famous actors both in the UK, America and around the world.

If you want to be an amazing actor, take a look at these references to learn how!

For Kids:

Drama 4 Kids
Free site with ideas for drama games and activities for kids.
http://drama4kids.com

Teach Wire
Drama games – Simple ideas for primary school
https://www.teachwire.net/news/8-drama-games-for-primary-kids-to-ignite-imagination/

Ice Breaker Ideas
15 Fun Drama Games For Kids (Theater & Acting)
https://icebreakerideas.com/drama-games-for-kids/

For parents and guardians:

How to Drama
Website detailing the accredited drama schools in the UK
https://howtodrama.com/accredited-drama-schools-uk/

National careers
National careers advice on a career in drama and acting.
https://nationalcareers.service.gov.uk/job-profiles/actor

Headshot Hunters
Advice on how to get children into acting.
https://headshothunter.co.uk/blog/getting-your-child-into-acting/

UCAS
UCAS advice on getting into performing arts in the UK
https://www.ucas.com/conservatoires/studying-conservatoire/thinking-about-performing-arts

What do you want to be when you grow up? Draw it below!

Notes!

Check out some other books in the series!

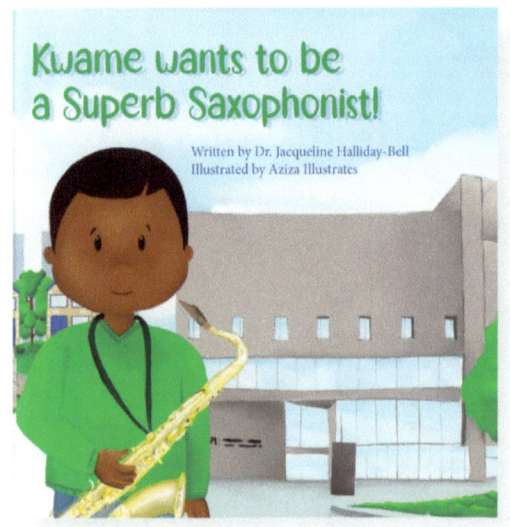
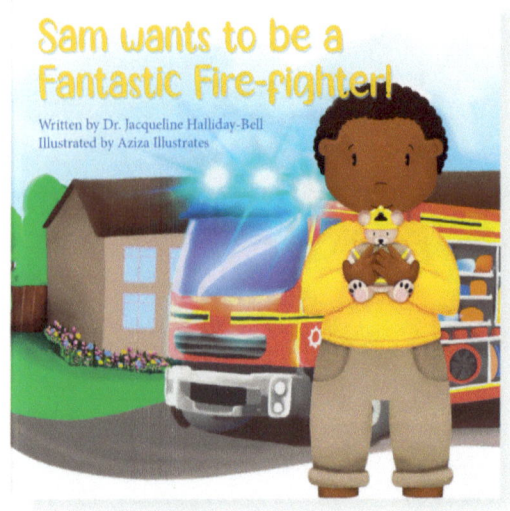

www.ingramcontent.com/pod-product-compliance
Lightning Source LLC
Chambersburg PA
CBHW041534040426
42446CB00002B/82